THE BROONS

Diary 2019

Week-to-view Diary
Vital Dates For 2019
Amazing Facts and Recipes
Broons Wisdom

Fun From the Happy Family that
Makes Every Family Happy

BLACK & WHITE PUBLISHING

Important Information

This diary belongs tae:

If Found, please return tae:

Tel:

In an emergency, please contact:

Mobile:

Home phone: Work phone:

Email: Work email:

Notes

2019

January

M	T	W	T	F	S	S
	1	2	3	4	5	6
7	8	9	10	11	12	13
14	15	16	17	18	19	20
21	22	23	24	25	26	27
28	29	30	31			

February

M	T	W	T	F	S	S
				1	2	3
4	5	6	7	8	9	10
11	12	13	14	15	16	17
18	19	20	21	22	23	24
25	26	27	28			

March

M	T	W	T	F	S	S
				1	2	3
4	5	6	7	8	9	10
11	12	13	14	15	16	17
18	19	20	21	22	23	24
25	26	27	28	29	30	31

April

M	T	W	T	F	S	S
1	2	3	4	5	6	7
8	9	10	11	12	13	14
15	16	17	18	19	20	21
22	23	24	25	26	27	28
29	30					

May

M	T	W	T	F	S	S
		1	2	3	4	5
6	7	8	9	10	11	12
13	14	15	16	17	18	19
20	21	22	23	24	25	26
27	28	29	30	31		

June

M	T	W	T	F	S	S
					1	2
3	4	5	6	7	8	9
10	11	12	13	14	15	16
17	18	19	20	21	22	23
24	25	26	27	28	29	30

July

M	T	W	T	F	S	S
1	2	3	4	5	6	7
8	9	10	11	12	13	14
15	16	17	18	19	20	21
22	23	24	25	26	27	28
29	30	31				

August

M	T	W	T	F	S	S
			1	2	3	4
5	6	7	8	9	10	11
12	13	14	15	16	17	18
19	20	21	22	23	24	25
26	27	28	29	30	31	

September

M	T	W	T	F	S	S
30						1
2	3	4	5	6	7	8
9	10	11	12	13	14	15
16	17	18	19	20	21	22
23	24	25	26	27	28	29

October

M	T	W	T	F	S	S
1	2	3	4	5	6	
7	8	9	10	11	12	13
14	15	16	17	18	19	20
21	22	23	24	25	26	27
28	29	30	31			

November

M	T	W	T	F	S	S
				1	2	3
4	5	6	7	8	9	10
11	12	13	14	15	16	17
18	19	20	21	22	23	24
25	26	27	28	29	30	

December

M	T	W	T	F	S	S
30	31					1
2	3	4	5	6	7	8
9	10	11	12	13	14	15
16	17	18	19	20	21	22
23	24	25	26	27	28	29

Notable Dates

JANUARY
Tuesday 1st	New Year's Day, holiday
Wednesday 2nd	Holiday (Scot)
Saturday 5th	Twelfth Night
Sunday 6th	Epiphany
Tuesday 15th	Makar Sankranti
Monday 21st	Martin Luther King, Jr. Day, holiday (US)
Friday 25th	Burns Night
Saturday 26th	Australia Day, holiday (Aus)
Sunday 27th	Holocaust Memorial Day (UK)

FEBRUARY
Saturday 2nd	Groundhog Day (Can, US)
Tuesday 5th	Chinese New Year (Year of the Pig)
Wednesday 6th	Waitangi Day, holiday (NZ)
Sunday 10th	Vasant Panchami
Thursday 14th	St. Valentine's Day
Monday 18th	Presidents' Day, holiday (US)

MARCH
Friday 1st	St. David's Day
Monday 4th	Maha Shivaratri
Tuesday 5th	Shrove Tuesday
Wednesday 6th	Ash Wednesday
Sunday 10th	Daylight Saving Time begins (US, Can)
Monday 11th	Commonwealth Day
Sunday 17th	St. Patrick's Day (R of I, NI)
Wednesday 20th	Holi begins at sunset
	Purim begins at sunset
Sunday 31st	Mother's Day (UK)
	British Summer Time begins

APRIL
Monday 1st	April Fool's Day
Saturday 6th	Tartan Day (Can, US)
Sunday 7th	Daylight Saving Time ends (NZ, Aus)
Tuesday 9th	Vimy Ridge Day (Can)
Sunday 14th	Rama Navami
Tuesday 16th	Emancipation Day
Friday 19th	Hanuman Jayanti
	Good Friday
	Passover begins at sunset
Sunday 21st	Easter Sunday
Monday 22nd	Easter Monday
Tuesday 23rd	St. George's Day
Thursday 25th	Anzac Day
Saturday 27th	Passover ends at sunset

MAY
Wednesday 1st	Holocaust Remembrance Day begins a sunset
Sunday 5th	Ramadan begins at sunset
Monday 6th	May Day, Early May Bank Holiday (UK)
Sunday 12th	Mother's Day (Aus, Can, NZ, US)
Monday 20th	Victoria Day
Sunday 26th	National Sorry Day (Aus)
Monday 27th	Spring Bank Holiday (UK, R of I)
	Memorial Day (US)
Thursday 30th	Ascension Day
Friday 31st	Laylat al-Qadr begins at sunset

JUNE
Tuesday 4th	Ramadan ends at sunset
	Eid al-Fitr begins at sunset
Saturday 8th	Shavuot begins at sunset
Sunday 9th	Pentecost
Monday 10th	Shavuot ends at sunset
Sunday 16th	Trinity Sunday
	Father's Day (UK, US, Can, R of I)
Thursday 20th	Corpus Christi
Friday 21st	Summer Solstice
	National Aboriginal Day (Can)
Monday 24th	St. John the Baptist Day

JULY
Monday 1st	Canada Day
Thursday 4th	Independence Day
Friday 12th	Battle of the Boyne (NI)
Monday 15th	St. Swithin's Day

AUGUST
Monday 5th	Civic Day (Can)
Saturday 10th	Tisha B'Av begins at sunset
Sunday 11th	Eid al-Adha begins at sunset
Thursday 15th	Eid al-Adha ends at sunset
Friday 23rd	Krishna Janmashtami
Monday 26th	Summer Bank Holiday (UK)
Saturday 31st	Muharram begins at sunset

SEPTEMBER
Sunday 1st	Father's Day (Aus, NZ)
	Ganesh Chaturthi begins
Monday 2nd	Labor Day (US)
Thursday 12th	Ganesh Chaturthi ends
Saturday 21st	International Day of Peace (United Nations)
Saturday 28th	Muharram ends at sunset
Sunday 29th	Rosh Hashanah begins at sunset
	New Zealand Daylight Saving Time begins
	Navratri begins

OCTOBER
Tuesday 1th	Rosh Hashanah ends at sunset
Sunday 6th	Australian Daylight Saving Time begins
Tuesday 8th	Yom Kippur begins at sunset
	Navratri ends
Thursday 10th	World Porridge Day
Sunday 13th	Sukkot begins at sunset
Monday 14th	Columbus Day (US)
Sunday 20th	Sukkot ends at sunset

Sunday 27th	British Summer Time ends
	Diwali begins
Thursday 31st	Hallowe'en
	Diwali ends

NOVEMBER
Friday 1st	All Saints' Day
Saturday 2nd	All Souls' Day
Sunday 3rd	Daylight Saving Time ends (US, Can)
Tuesday 5th	Guy Fawkes Night (UK)
Sunday 10th	Remembrance Sunday
Monday 11th	Remembrance Day
	Veterans Day (US)
Wednesday 13th	Robert Louis Stevenson Day
Thursday 28th	Thanksgiving Day (US)
Saturday 30th	St. Andrew's Day

DECEMBER
Sunday 1st	Advent Sunday
Tuesday 10th	Human Rights Day
Sunday 22nd	Hanukkah begins at sunset
	Winter Solstice
Tuesday 24th	Christmas Eve
Wednesday 25th	Christmas Day, holiday
Thursday 26th	Boxing Day, holiday
Monday 30th	Hanukkah ends at sunset
Tuesday 31st	Hogmanay (New Year's Eve)

Famous Scots'

JANUARY
1st   Paul Lawrie (1969) – Open Golf Champion 1999
3rd   Gavin Hastings (1962) – former Scottish Rugby Captain
6th   John Byrne (1940) – Playwright/Artist
9th   Paulo Nutini (1987) – Singer/Songwriter
11th   John Sessions (1953) – Actor/Comedian (real name John Marshall)
12th   Nick Nairn (1959) – Celebrity Chef
13th   Stephen Hendry (1969) – World Snooker Champion
17th   Calvin Harris (1984) – DJ/Record Producer/Singer (real name Adam Wilesh)
18th   Willie Collum (1979) – Football Referee
27th   Alan Cumming (1965) – Actor

FEBRUARY
9th   Gordon Strachan (1957) – Footballer/Manager
12th   Annette Crosbie (1934) – Actor
20th   Gordon Brown (1951) – former Prime Minister
23rd   Kelly Macdonald (1976) – Actor
24th   Denis Law (1940) – Footballer

MARCH
4th   Kenny Dalglish (1951) – Footballer/Manager
5th   Craig and Charlie Reid (1962) – The Proclaimers
7th   Tommy Sheridan (1964) – Politician
8th   David Wilkie (1954) – Olympic Gold Medal Swimmer 1976
23rd   Sir Chris Hoy (1976) –Six time Olympic Gold Medal Cyclist (2004/2008/2012)
23rd   Marti Pellow (1965) – Singer/Songwriter (real name Mark McLachlan)
30th   Robbie Coltrane (1950) – Actor/Comedian (real name Anthony McMillan)
31st   Ewan McGregor (1971) – Actor

APRIL
1st   Susan Boyle (1961) – Singer
10th   Nicky Campbell (1961) – TV Presenter

14th   Robert Carlyle (1961) – Actor
14th   James McFadden (1983) – Footballer
14th   Peter Capaldi (1958) – Actor
18th   David Tennant (1971) – Actor (real name David McDonald)
21st   James McAvoy (1979) – Actor
21st   Tam Cowan (1969) – Football Broadcaster
23rd   John Hannah (1962) – Actor
27th   Sheena Easton (1959) – Singer (born Sheena Or
30th   Sam Heughan (1980) – Actor

MAY
3rd   Allan Wells (1952) – Olympic 100 Metres Gold Medalist in 1980
4th   Chick Young (1951) – Football pundit
6th   Tony Blair (1963) – former Prime Minister
6th   Graeme Souness (1953) – Footballer/Manager
9th   Laura Muir (1993) – Athlete
10th   Donovan Leitch (1946) – Singer/Songwriter
15th   Sir Andy Murray (1987) – Tennis Player. Olympic Champion 2012, 2016
18th   John Higgins (1975) – World Snooker Champion
24th   Liz McColgan (1964) – Athlete/BBC Sports Personality of the Year in 1991
29th   Carol Kirkwood (1962) – BBC Weather Presenter

JUNE
1st   Brian Cox (1946) – Actor
3rd   Bill Paterson (1945) – Actor
4th   Val McDermid (1955) – Crime Writer
6th   Kyle Falconer (1987) – Singer/Songwriter
11th   Jackie Stewart (1939) – Formula 1 Champion
13th   Alan Hansen (1955) – Footballer/Commentator
18th   Richard Madden (1986) – Actor
23rd   K. T. Tunstall (1975) – Singer/Songwriter
23rd   Colin Montgomerie (1963) – Golfer
24th   Stuart Hogg (1992) – Rugby Player
25th   Scott Brown (1985) – Footballer
28th   Ken Buchanan (1945) – World Boxing Champion

Birthdays

JLY
h   Richard Wilson (1936) – Actor
h   Jim Kerr (1959) – Singer/Songwriter
th   Lindsey Sharp (1990) – Athlete
th   Nina Nesbitt (1994) – Singer/Songwriter
3th Jim Watt (1948) – World Champion Boxer
9th Nicola Sturgeon (1970) – First Minister of Scotland
0th Nicola Benedetti (1987) – Classical Violinist
1st J. K. Rowling (1965) – Author
1st Jackie Bird (1962) – Journalist/Newsreader

UGUST
nd   Elaine C. Smith (1958) – Actor
th   Katie Leung (1987) – Actor
1th Ashley Jensen (1969) – Actor
4th Sam Torrance (1953) – Golfer/Commentator
5th Sir Sean Connery (1930) – Actor
5th Amy MacDonald (1987) – Singer/Songwriter
5th Catriona Matthew (1969) – Major Golf Champion 2009
7th Denis Lawson (1947) – Actor

EPTEMBER
th   Al Stewart (1945) – Singer/Songwriter
th   Christopher Brookmyre (1968) – Author
1th Graeme Obree (1965) – Champion Cyclist
1th John Greig (1942) – Footballer/Manager
6th Andy Irvine (1951) – Rugby Player
4th Ally McCoist (1962) – Footballer/Manager/TV Personality
7th Barbara Dickson (1947) – Singer/Actor
7th Irvine Welsh (1958) – Author

CTOBER
nd   John Robertson (1964) – Footballer/Manager
2th Greig Laidlaw (1985) – Rugby Player
2th Rhona Martin (1966) – Olympic Champion Curler 2002

14th   Sir David Murray (1951) – Businessman
19th   Ken Stott (1954) – Actor
22nd   Craig Levein (1964) – Footballer/Manager

NOVEMBER
3rd   Lulu (1948) – Singer/Actress (real name Marie Lawrie)
5th   Tilda Swinton (1960) – Actor
6th   Susan Calman (1974) – Comedian/TV Presenter
7th   Sharleen Spiteri (1967) – Singer/Songwriter
8th   Gordon Ramsay (1966) – Celebrity Chef
10th   Ruth Davidson (1978) – Politician
12th   Stuart Cosgrove (1952) – Journalist/Broadcaster
13th   Kevin Bridges (1986) – Comedian
13th   Gerard Butler (1969) – Actor
16th   Willie Carson (1942) – Jockey/TV Personality
17th   Jack Vettriano (1951) – Artist (real name Jack Hoggan)
23rd   Kirsty Young (1968) – TV and Radio Presenter
24th   Sir Billy Connolly (1942) – Comedian/Musician/ Actor
25th   Dougray Scott (1965) – Actor
28th   Karen Gillan (1987) – Actor/Director/Screenwriter
30th   Lorraine Kelly (1969) – TV Presenter

DECEMBER
1st   Anita Manning (1947) - Antiques Expert/TV Personality
11th   Justin Currie (1964) – Singer/Songwriter
22nd   Ricky Ross (1957) – Singer/Songwriter/ Broadcaster
25th   Annie Lennox (1964) – Singer/Songwriter
31st   Alex Salmond (1954) – former First Minister of Scotland
31st   Sir Alex Ferguson (1941) – Footballer/Manager

Clothing Sizes

WOMEN'S CLOTHING SIZE

UK	4	6	8	10	12	14	16	18	20	22	24
US	0	2	4	6	8	10	12	14	16	18	20
EU	32	34	36	38	40	42	44	46	48	50	52

GIRLS' DRESSES AND COATS

UK	3	5	7	9	11	13	15	17
US	1	3	5	7	9	11	13	15
EU	28	30	32	34	36	38	40	42

MEN'S SUITS, JUMPERS AND COATS

UK/US	38	40	42	44	46	48	50	52	54
EU	48	50	52	54	56	58	60	62	64

MEN'S SHIRTS

	S	M	L	XL	XXL	3XL	4XL
UK/US	14-14½	15-15½	16-16½	17-17½	18-18½	19-19½	20-20½
EU	36	38-40	42-44	46-48	50-52	54-56	58-60

HAT SIZES

UK	6⅜	6½	6⅝	6¾	6⅞	7	7⅛	7¼	7⅜	7½	7⅝
US	6½	6⅝	6¾	6⅞	7	7⅛	7¼	7⅜	7½	7⅝	7¾
Inches	20½	20⅞	21¼	21⅝	22	22½	22⅞	23¼	23⅝	24	24½
Centimetres	52	53	54	55	56	57	58	59	60	61	62

& Conversions

WOMEN'S SHOES

UK	2	2.5	3	3.5	4	4.5	5	5.5	6	6.5	7	7.5	8
US	4.5	5	5.5	6	6.5	7	7.5	8	8.5	9	9.5	10	10.5
EU	34	35	35.5	36	37	37.5	38	38.5	39	39.5	40	41	42

MEN'S SHOES

UK	5	5.5	6	6.5	7	7.5	8	8.5	9	9.5	10	10.5	11	11.5	12
US	5.5	6	6.5	7	7.5	8	8.5	9	9.5	10	10.5	11	11.5	12	12.5
EU	38	38.7	39.3	40	40.5	41	42	42.5	43	44	44.5	45	46	46.5	47

GIRLS' SHOES

UK	8	8.5	9	9.5	10	10.5	11	11.5	12	12.5	13	13.5	1	1.5	2	2.5
US	8.5	9	9.5	10	10.5	11	11.5	12	13.5	1	1.5	2	2.5	3	3.5	4
EU	26	26.5	27	27.5	28	28.5	29	30	30.5	31	31.5	32.2	33	33.5	34	35

BOYS' SHOES

UK	11	11.5	12	12.5	13	13.5	1	1.5	2	2.5	3	3.5	4	4.5
US	11.5	12	12.5	13	13.5	1	1.5	2	2.5	3	3.5	4	4.5	5
EU	29	29.7	30.5	31	31.5	33	33.5	34	34.7	35	35.5	36	37	37.5

THE BROONS

WATTY

D C THOMSON & CO LTD GLASGOW, DUNDEE AND LONDON

A

January

Each New Year's Eve, the family play
Charades – a word they're guessin'.
While Maw and Paw look in dismay,
The bairns teach them a lesson.

December / January

31 Monday

1 Tuesday
New Year's Day, holiday

2 Wednesday
Holiday (Scot)

January

3 Thursday

4 Friday

5 Saturday

Twelfth Night

6 Sunday

Epiphany

Wk	M	T	W	T	F	S	S
1		1	2	3	4	5	6
2	7	8	9	10	11	12	13
3	14	15	16	17	18	19	20
4	21	22	23	24	25	26	27
5	28	29	30	31			

January

7 Monday

8 Tuesday

9 Wednesday

January

10 Thursday

_____
_____
_____
_____
_____
_____
_____
_____
_____
_____
_____
_____
_____
_____
_____
_____
_____
_____
_____
_____
_____
_____
_____
_____

11 Friday

_____
_____
_____
_____
_____
_____
_____
_____
_____
_____
_____
_____
_____
_____
_____
_____
_____
_____
_____
_____
_____
_____
_____
_____

12 Saturday

_____
_____
_____
_____
_____
_____
_____

13 Sunday

_____
_____
_____
_____
_____
_____
_____
_____
_____
_____
_____

Wk	M	T	W	T	F	S	S
1		1	2	3	4	5	6
2	7	8	9	10	11	12	13
3	14	15	16	17	18	19	20
4	21	22	23	24	25	26	27
5	28	29	30	31			

January

14 Monday

15 Tuesday

Makar Sankranti

16 Wednesday

January

17 Thursday

18 Friday

19 Saturday

20 Sunday

Wk	M	T	W	T	F	S	S
1		1	2	3	4	5	6
2	7	8	9	10	11	12	13
3	14	15	16	17	18	19	20
4	21	22	23	24	25	26	27
5	28	29	30	31			

January

21 Monday

Martin Luther King, Jr. Day, holiday (US)

22 Tuesday

23 Wednesday

January

24 Thursday

25 Friday

Burns Night

26 Saturday

Australia Day, holiday (Aus)

27 Sunday

Holocaust Memorial Day (UK)

Wk	M	T	W	T	F	S	S
1		1	2	3	4	5	6
2	7	8	9	10	11	12	13
3	14	15	16	17	18	19	20
4	21	22	23	24	25	26	27
5	28	29	30	31			

January

28 Monday

29 Tuesday

30 Wednesday

February

Winter's grand for parlour games,
So dignified and quiet.
That may have been the Family's aims –
The outcome – one huge riot!

FAITHERS O' INVENTION

MACKINTOSH RUBBERISED RAINCOATS
Invented by Glaswegian Charles Macintosh (1766 – 1843)

January / February

31 Thursday

1 Friday

2 Saturday

Groundhog Day (Can, US)

3 Sunday

Wk	M	T	W	T	F	S	S
5					1	2	3
6	4	5	6	7	8	9	10
7	11	12	13	14	15	16	17
8	18	19	20	21	22	23	24
9	25	26	27	28			

February

4 Monday

5 Tuesday

Chinese New Year (Year of the Pig)

6 Wednesday

Waitangi Day, holiday (NZ)

February

7 Thursday

8 Friday

9 Saturday

10 Sunday

Vasant Panchami

Wk	M	T	W	T	F	S	S
5					1	2	3
6	4	5	6	7	8	9	10
7	11	12	13	14	15	16	17
8	18	19	20	21	22	23	24
9	25	26	27	28			

February

11 Monday

12 Tuesday

13 Wednesday

February

14 Thursday

St. Valentine's Day

15 Friday

16 Saturday

17 Sunday

Wk	M	T	W	T	F	S	S
5					1	2	3
6	4	5	6	7	8	9	10
7	11	12	13	14	15	16	17
8	18	19	20	21	22	23	24
9	25	26	27	28			

February

18 Monday

Presidents' Day, holiday (US)

19 Tuesday

20 Wednesday

February

21 Thursday

22 Friday

23 Saturday

24 Sunday

Wk	M	T	W	T	F	S	S
5					1	2	3
6	4	5	6	7	8	9	10
7	11	12	13	14	15	16	17
8	18	19	20	21	22	23	24
9	25	26	27	28			

February

25 Monday

26 Tuesday

27 Wednesday

March

The menfowk help on Mither's Day.
They slave away for hours.
Maw has it tough, they have to say...
Next year they'll buy her flowers!

MAW BROON'S RECIPES

Tattie Scones

YE'LL NEED:

450g (1lb) o' boiled tatties

130g (5oz) o' flour

6 tablespoons o' melted butter

A teaspoonful o' salt

A thick bottomed frying pan and a small plate (Keep hud o' these – ye'll need them for another recipe later in the diary)

WHIT TAE DAE:

1. Mash up the boiled tatties while still warm and add the butter and salt.
2. Add enough flour tae mak a nice pliable dough but watch it doesn't get ower dry.
3. Turn out onto a floured board and roll oot to a ¼ inch thickness. Using the small plate, cut the dough into circles and then quarter these wi' a knife (dinna cut right through). Prick all over wi' a fork. Cook in yer lightly greased frying pan for aboot three minutes per side (until golden brown). Ye'll need tae cook each one separately.

"Paw loves these if I put a slice o' cheese between twa scones and heat further until the cheese melts – BRAWSOME!"

February / March

28 Thursday

1 Friday

St. David's Day

2 Saturday

3 Sunday

Wk	M	T	W	T	F	S	S
9					1	2	3
10	4	5	6	7	8	9	10
11	11	12	13	14	15	16	17
12	18	19	20	21	22	23	24
13	25	26	27	28	29	30	31

March

4 Monday

Maha Shivaratri

5 Tuesday

Shrove Tuesday

6 Wednesday

Ash Wednesday

March

7 Thursday

_____
_____
_____
_____
_____
_____
_____
_____
_____
_____
_____
_____
_____
_____
_____
_____
_____
_____
_____
_____
_____
_____
_____
_____
_____
_____

8 Friday

_____
_____
_____
_____
_____
_____
_____
_____
_____
_____
_____
_____
_____
_____
_____
_____
_____
_____
_____
_____
_____
_____
_____
_____

9 Saturday

_____
_____
_____
_____
_____
_____
_____
_____
_____
_____

10 Sunday

Daylight Saving Time begins (US, Can)

_____
_____
_____
_____
_____
_____
_____
_____
_____
_____
_____

Wk	M	T	W	T	F	S	S
9					1	2	3
10	4	5	6	7	8	9	10
11	11	12	13	14	15	16	17
12	18	19	20	21	22	23	24
13	25	26	27	28	29	30	31

March

11 Monday

Commonwealth Day

12 Tuesday

13 Wednesday

March

14 **Thursday**

15 **Friday**

16 **Saturday**

17 **Sunday**

St. Patrick's Day (R of I, NI)

Wk	M	T	W	T	F	S	S
9					1	2	3
10	4	5	6	7	8	9	10
11	11	12	13	14	15	16	17
12	18	19	20	21	22	23	24
13	25	26	27	28	29	30	31

March

18 Monday

19 Tuesday

20 Wednesday

Holi begins at sunset

Purim begins at sunset

March

21 Thursday

22 Friday

23 Saturday

24 Sunday

Wk	M	T	W	T	F	S	S
9					1	2	3
10	4	5	6	7	8	9	10
11	11	12	13	14	15	16	17
12	18	19	20	21	22	23	24
13	25	26	27	28	29	30	31

March

25 Monday

26 Tuesday

27 Wednesday

March

28 Thursday

29 Friday

30 Saturday

31 Sunday

Mother's Day (UK)

British Summer Time begins

Wk	M	T	W	T	F	S	S
9					1	2	3
10	4	5	6	7	8	9	10
11	11	12	13	14	15	16	17
12	18	19	20	21	22	23	24
13	25	26	27	28	29	30	31

FAITHERS O' INVENTION

MACADAMISED ROADS
Invented by Ayr man, John Loudon McAdam
(1756 – 1836) around 1800.

April

Look at Paw he's in a state.
He really should keep cool.
Just a minute – check the date...
He's such an April Fool

April

1 Monday

April Fool's Day

2 Tuesday

3 Wednesday

April

4 Thursday

_____
_____
_____
_____
_____
_____
_____
_____
_____
_____
_____
_____
_____
_____
_____
_____
_____
_____
_____
_____
_____
_____
_____

5 Friday

_____
_____
_____
_____
_____
_____
_____
_____
_____
_____
_____
_____
_____
_____
_____
_____
_____
_____
_____
_____
_____
_____

6 Saturday

Tartan Day (Can, US)

_____
_____
_____
_____
_____
_____

7 Sunday

Daylight Saving Time ends (NZ, Aus)

_____
_____
_____
_____
_____
_____
_____
_____

Wk	M	T	W	T	F	S	S
14	1	2	3	4	5	6	7
15	8	9	10	11	12	13	14
16	15	16	17	18	19	20	21
17	22	23	24	25	26	27	28
18	29	30					

8 Monday

9 Tuesday

Vimy Ridge Day (Can)

10 Wednesday

April

11 Thursday

_____
_____
_____
_____
_____
_____
_____
_____
_____
_____
_____
_____
_____
_____
_____
_____
_____
_____
_____
_____
_____
_____
_____

12 Friday

_____
_____
_____
_____
_____
_____
_____
_____
_____
_____
_____
_____
_____
_____
_____
_____
_____
_____
_____
_____
_____

13 Saturday

_____
_____
_____
_____
_____
_____
_____
_____

14 Sunday

Rama Navami

_____
_____
_____
_____
_____
_____
_____
_____
_____

Wk	M	T	W	T	F	S	S
14	1	2	3	4	5	6	7
15	8	9	10	11	12	13	14
16	15	16	17	18	19	20	21
17	22	23	24	25	26	27	28
18	29	30					

April

15 Monday

16 Tuesday

Emancipation Day

17 Wednesday

April

18 Thursday

_____
_____
_____
_____
_____
_____
_____
_____
_____
_____
_____
_____
_____
_____
_____
_____
_____
_____
_____
_____
_____
_____
_____
_____
_____
_____
_____
_____

19 Friday

Hanuman Jayanti

Good Friday

Passover begins at sunset

_____
_____
_____
_____
_____
_____
_____
_____
_____
_____
_____
_____
_____
_____
_____
_____
_____
_____
_____
_____
_____
_____
_____

20 Saturday

_____
_____
_____
_____
_____
_____
_____
_____

21 Sunday

Easter Sunday

_____
_____
_____
_____
_____
_____
_____
_____
_____

Wk	M	T	W	T	F	S	S
14	1	2	3	4	5	6	7
15	8	9	10	11	12	13	14
16	15	16	17	18	19	20	21
17	22	23	24	25	26	27	28
18	29	30					

April

22 Monday

Easter Monday

23 Tuesday

St. George's Day

24 Wednesday

25 Thursday

nzac Day

_____

_____

_____

_____

_____

_____

_____

_____

_____

_____

_____

_____

_____

_____

_____

_____

_____

_____

_____

_____

_____

_____

_____

26 Friday

_____

_____

_____

_____

_____

_____

_____

_____

_____

_____

_____

_____

_____

_____

_____

_____

_____

_____

_____

_____

_____

27 Saturday

Passover ends at sunset

_____

_____

_____

_____

_____

_____

_____

_____

_____

28 Sunday

_____

_____

_____

_____

_____

_____

_____

_____

_____

Wk	M	T	W	T	F	S	S
14	1	2	3	4	5	6	7
15	8	9	10	11	12	13	14
16	15	16	17	18	19	20	21
17	22	23	24	25	26	27	28
18	29	30					

April / May

29 Monday

30 Tuesday

1 Wednesday

Holocaust Remembrance Day

begins at sunset

May

Horace needs the noise to cease
For his examination.
But he would hae a lot mair peace
In Glasgow Central Station.

WID YE BELIEVE IT?

Horace's Amazing Facts

HORACE
AN INDIAN MAN WAS BORN WI' 14 FINGERS AND 20 TOES.

TWIN
"LUCKY DEVIL – THAT WOULD MAK SUMS SO MUCH EASIER!"

HORACE
THE WORLD'S TALLEST MAN EVER WIS ROBERT PERSHING WADLOW FROM THE USA. HE WIS 8FT 11INS TALL IN 1940.

HEN
"JINGS! MAKS ME LOOK LIKE A WEE SKELF!"

HORACE
A CAR NUMBER PLATE SHOWING ONLY THE NUMBER '1' WAS BOUGHT FOR 7.2 MILLION POUNDS BY SOMEONE FROM THE UNITED ARAB EMIRATES.

DAPHNE
"WHIT IF THE NUMBER GOT SAND-BLASTED AFF IN A SANDSTORM?!"

HORACE
SCOTLAND IS HAME TAE THE SHORTEST PLACE NAME IN BRITAIN: AE.

MAGGIE
"JUST LIKE GRAN'PAW SAYS WHEN HE CAN'T HEAR YOU!"

May

2 Thursday

_____
_____
_____
_____
_____
_____
_____
_____
_____
_____
_____
_____
_____
_____
_____
_____
_____
_____
_____
_____
_____
_____
_____
_____
_____
_____

3 Friday

_____
_____
_____
_____
_____
_____
_____
_____
_____
_____
_____
_____
_____
_____
_____
_____
_____
_____
_____

4 Saturday

_____
_____
_____
_____
_____
_____
_____
_____

5 Sunday

Ramadan begins at sunset
_____
_____
_____
_____
_____
_____
_____
_____
_____

Wk	M	T	W	T	F	S	S
18		1	2	3	4	5
19	6	7	8	9	10	11	12
20	13	14	15	16	17	18	19
21	20	21	22	23	24	25	26
22	27	28	29	30	31

May

6 Monday

May Day, Early May Bank Holiday (UK)

7 Tuesday

8 Wednesday

May

9 Thursday

_____
_____
_____
_____
_____
_____
_____
_____
_____
_____
_____
_____
_____
_____
_____
_____
_____
_____
_____
_____
_____
_____
_____
_____
_____
_____
_____

10 Friday

_____
_____
_____
_____
_____
_____
_____
_____
_____
_____
_____
_____
_____
_____
_____
_____
_____
_____
_____
_____
_____
_____

11 Saturday

_____
_____
_____
_____
_____
_____
_____
_____
_____

12 Sunday

Mother's Day (Aus, Can, NZ, US)

_____
_____
_____
_____
_____
_____
_____
_____

Wk	M	T	W	T	F	S	S
18			1	2	3	4	5
19	6	7	8	9	10	11	12
20	13	14	15	16	17	18	19
21	20	21	22	23	24	25	26
22	27	28	29	30	31		

May

13 Monday

14 Tuesday

15 Wednesday

May

16 Thursday

_____
_____
_____
_____
_____
_____
_____
_____
_____
_____
_____
_____
_____
_____
_____
_____
_____
_____
_____
_____
_____
_____
_____
_____

17 Friday

_____
_____
_____
_____
_____
_____
_____
_____
_____
_____
_____
_____
_____
_____
_____
_____
_____

18 Saturday

_____
_____
_____
_____
_____
_____
_____

19 Sunday

_____
_____
_____
_____
_____
_____
_____
_____
_____

Wk	M	T	W	T	F	S	S
18			1	2	3	4	5
19	6	7	8	9	10	11	12
20	13	14	15	16	17	18	19
21	20	21	22	23	24	25	26
22	27	28	29	30	31		

May

20 Monday

Victoria Day

21 Tuesday

22 Wednesday

May

23 Thursday

24 Friday

25 Saturday

26 Sunday

National Sorry Day (Aus)

Wk	M	T	W	T	F	S	S
18		1	2	3	4	5
19	6	7	8	9	10	11	12
20	13	14	15	16	17	18	19
21	20	21	22	23	24	25	26
22	27	28	29	30	31		

May

27 Monday

Spring Bank Holiday (UK, R of I)

Memorial Day (US)

28 Tuesday

29 Wednesday

June

A day oot in a car tae see
The site o' glorious battles.
But for Paw that's no' tae be -
He's grounded fixing rattles!

FANCY A SUMMER FESTIVAL?

WIFE CARRYING WORLD CHAMPIONSHIPS – FINLAND in JULY

Husbands race down an obstacle-strewn track of about 300 yards carrying their wife (or someone else's wife) round their neck. The favoured method is for the wife to cross her legs round her partner's throat hanging on to his back.

"Michty! A maw 'scarf' wid just aboot feenish me aff!"

YORKSHIRE PUDDING BOAT RACE – YORKSHIRE in JUNE

In Brawby, Yorkshire, they have an annual boat race using vessels made from giant yorkshire puddings covered with several coats of yacht varnish (to stop them going soggy).

"Ye'd need a whole coo to mak enough roast beef to go wi' thae Yorkshire puds."

BORYEONG MUD FESTIVAL – SOUTH KOREA in JULY

Mud sculptures, mud mazes, mudslides, even a mud prison are all part of this weird festival using the theraputic local mud.

"The twins wid enjoy that – ye should see the state they get intae playin' fitba at Bogside Park."

AIR GUITAR FESTIVAL FINLAND in AUGUST

Would-be rock stars make their moves and strum their imaginary fender stratocasters in this fun festival.

"Maybe we could hae an air bagpipe festival in Scotland!"

May / June

30 Thursday

Ascension Day

_____

_____

_____

_____

_____

_____

_____

_____

_____

_____

_____

_____

_____

_____

_____

_____

_____

_____

_____

_____

_____

_____

31 Friday

Laylat al-Qadr begins at sunset

_____

_____

_____

_____

_____

_____

_____

_____

_____

_____

_____

_____

_____

_____

_____

_____

_____

_____

_____

_____

_____

1 Saturday

_____

_____

_____

_____

_____

_____

_____

_____

2 Sunday

_____

_____

_____

_____

_____

_____

_____

_____

_____

Wk	M	T	W	T	F	S	S
22						1	2
23	3	4	5	6	7	8	9
24	10	11	12	13	14	15	16
25	17	18	19	20	21	22	23
26	24	25	26	27	28	29	30

June

3 Monday

4 Tuesday

Ramadan ends at sunset

Eid al-Fitr begins at sunset

5 Wednesday

June

6 Thursday

7 Friday

8 Saturday

Shavuot begins at sunset

9 Sunday

Pentecost

Wk	M	T	W	T	F	S	S
22						1	2
23	3	4	5	6	7	8	9
24	10	11	12	13	14	15	16
25	17	18	19	20	21	22	23
26	24	25	26	27	28	29	30

June

10 Monday

Shavuot ends at sunset

11 Tuesday

12 Wednesday

June

13 Thursday

14 Friday

15 Saturday

16 Sunday

Trinity Sunday

Father's Day (UK, US, Can, R of I)

Wk	M	T	W	T	F	S	S
22						1	2
23	3	4	5	6	7	8	9
24	10	11	12	13	14	15	16
25	17	18	19	20	21	22	23
26	24	25	26	27	28	29	30

June

17 Monday

18 Tuesday

19 Wednesday

June

20 Thursday

orpus Christi

_____

_____

_____

_____

_____

_____

_____

_____

_____

_____

_____

_____

_____

_____

_____

_____

_____

_____

_____

_____

_____

_____

21 Friday

Summer Solstice

_____

National Aboriginal Day (Can)

_____

_____

_____

_____

_____

_____

_____

_____

_____

_____

_____

_____

_____

_____

_____

_____

22 Saturday

_____

_____

_____

_____

_____

_____

_____

_____

_____

23 Sunday

_____

_____

_____

_____

_____

_____

_____

_____

_____

Wk	M	T	W	T	F	S	S
22						1	2
23	3	4	5	6	7	8	9
24	10	11	12	13	14	15	16
25	17	18	19	20	21	22	23
26	24	25	26	27	28	29	30

June

24 Monday

St. John the Baptist Day

25 Tuesday

26 Wednesday

June

27 Thursday

28 Friday

29 Saturday

30 Sunday

Wk	M	T	W	T	F	S	S
22						1	2
23	3	4	5	6	7	8	9
24	10	11	12	13	14	15	16
25	17	18	19	20	21	22	23
26	24	25	26	27	28	29	30

FAITHERS O' INVENTION

GAS STREET LIGHTING
Was invented by William Murdoch (1754 – 1839)
of Cumnock in the early 1790s.

July

The bairns are playin' on the swings.
The auld lads want a shottie.
And soon they're flyin' like they've wings –
I hope they don't get caught, eh?

July

1 Monday

Canada Day

2 Tuesday

3 Wednesday

July

4 Thursday

Independence Day

5 Friday

6 Saturday

7 Sunday

Wk	M	T	W	T	F	S	S
27	1	2	3	4	5	6	7
28	8	9	10	11	12	13	14
29	15	16	17	18	19	20	21
30	22	23	24	25	26	27	28
31	29	30	31				

July

8 Monday

9 Tuesday

10 Wednesday

July

1 Thursday

_____
_____
_____
_____
_____
_____
_____
_____
_____
_____
_____
_____
_____
_____
_____
_____
_____
_____
_____
_____
_____
_____
_____
_____
_____
_____

12 Friday

Battle of the Boyne (NI)

_____
_____
_____
_____
_____
_____
_____
_____
_____
_____
_____
_____
_____
_____
_____
_____
_____
_____
_____
_____
_____
_____

13 Saturday

_____
_____
_____
_____
_____
_____
_____
_____
_____

14 Sunday

_____
_____
_____
_____
_____
_____
_____
_____
_____
_____
_____
_____
_____
_____

Wk	M	T	W	T	F	S	S
27	1	2	3	4	5	6	7
28	8	9	10	11	12	13	14
29	15	16	17	18	19	20	21
30	22	23	24	25	26	27	28
31	29	30	31				

July

15 Monday

St. Swithin's Day

16 Tuesday

17 Wednesday

July

8 Thursday

19 Friday

20 Saturday

21 Sunday

Wk	M	T	W	T	F	S	S
27	1	2	3	4	5	6	7
28	8	9	10	11	12	13	14
29	15	16	17	18	19	20	21
30	22	23	24	25	26	27	28
31	29	30	31				

July

22 Monday

23 Tuesday

24 Wednesday

July

25 Thursday

26 Friday

27 Saturday

28 Sunday

Wk	M	T	W	T	F	S	S
27	1	2	3	4	5	6	7
28	8	9	10	11	12	13	14
29	15	16	17	18	19	20	21
30	22	23	24	25	26	27	28
31	29	30	31				

July

29 Monday

30 Tuesday

31 Wednesday

August

The Broons are giein' gowf a turn –
At least that is their mission.
They dig up worms, land in the burn –
They should have a' gone fishin'!

MAW BROON'S RECIPES

Traditional Scottish Bannocks

YE'LL NEED:

250g (8ozs) o' medium oatmeal

4 teaspoons o' melted bacon fat

4 pinches o' bicarbonate of soda

Good pinch o' salt

1 ½ teaspoons o' hot water

Some mair oatmeal for kneading

The kitchen utensils, small plate and heavy pan ye used for the tattie scones

WHIT TAE DAE:

1. Mix up the oatmeal, salt and bicarbonate of soda in a bowl and pour the melted fat intae the middle o' the mixture.
2. Stir well, using a wooden spoon then add in enough hot water tae mak a stiff paste.
3. Cover a large plate or board wi' oatmeal and plonk yer mixture on this. Work quickly as the paste is difficult to work wi' when it cools.
4. Divide intae four and roll the first one intae a ball wi yer hands covered in oatmeal.
5. Roll out till aboot ¼ inch thick then use yer plate tae cut intae a circle. Next quarter that circle wi' a knife.
6. Place in preheated, lightly-greased pan and cook for around three minutes per side. Ye'll ken when it's ready tae turn, cos the edges curl up a wee bit.
7. Do the same wi' yer other three balls o' mixture.

"Perfect wi' soup or stovies"

August

1 Thursday

_____
_____
_____
_____
_____
_____
_____
_____
_____
_____
_____
_____
_____
_____
_____
_____
_____
_____
_____
_____
_____
_____
_____
_____
_____

2 Friday

_____
_____
_____
_____
_____
_____
_____
_____
_____
_____
_____
_____
_____
_____
_____
_____
_____
_____
_____
_____
_____
_____

3 Saturday

_____
_____
_____
_____
_____
_____
_____
_____
_____

4 Sunday

_____
_____
_____
_____
_____
_____
_____
_____
_____
_____

Wk	M	T	W	T	F	S	S
31				1	2	3	4
32	5	6	7	8	9	10	11
33	12	13	14	15	16	17	18
34	19	20	21	22	23	24	25
35	26	27	28	29	30	31	

5 Monday

Civic Day (Can)

6 Tuesday

7 Wednesday

August

8 Thursday

_____
_____
_____
_____
_____
_____
_____
_____
_____
_____
_____
_____
_____
_____
_____
_____
_____
_____
_____
_____
_____
_____
_____
_____
_____
_____

9 Friday

_____
_____
_____
_____
_____
_____
_____
_____
_____
_____
_____
_____
_____
_____
_____
_____
_____
_____
_____
_____
_____
_____
_____
_____

10 Saturday

Tisha B'Av begins at sunset

_____
_____
_____
_____
_____
_____
_____
_____

11 Sunday

Eid al-Adha begins at sunset

_____
_____
_____
_____
_____
_____
_____
_____

Wk	M	T	W	T	F	S	S
31				1	2	3	4
32	5	6	7	8	9	10	11
33	12	13	14	15	16	17	18
34	19	20	21	22	23	24	25
35	26	27	28	29	30	31	

August

12 Monday

13 Tuesday

14 Wednesday

August

5 Thursday

al-Adha ends at sunset

16 Friday

17 Saturday

18 Sunday

Wk	M	T	W	T	F	S	S
31			1	2	3	4	
32	5	6	7	8	9	10	11
33	12	13	14	15	16	17	18
34	19	20	21	22	23	24	25
35	26	27	28	29	30	31	

August

19 Monday

20 Tuesday

21 Wednesday

August

22 Thursday

23 Friday

Krishna Janmashtami

24 Saturday

25 Sunday

Wk	M	T	W	T	F	S	S
31				1	2	3	4
32	5	6	7	8	9	10	11
33	12	13	14	15	16	17	18
34	19	20	21	22	23	24	25
35	26	27	28	29	30	31	

August

26 Monday

Summer Bank Holiday (UK)

27 Tuesday

28 Wednesday

September

The lads got drookit at the game.
The day was far from fair.
Maw winnae let them in their hame
Tae dreep on her clean flair!

FAITHERS O' INVENTION

ANTIBIOTICS
Were invented in 1928 by Alexander Fleming (1881 – 1955)
near Darvel in Ayrshire.

August / September

29 Thursday

30 Friday

31 Saturday

Muharram begins at sunset

1 Sunday

Father's Day (Aus, NZ)

Ganesh Chaturthi begins

Wk	M	T	W	T	F	S	S
35							1
36	2	3	4	5	6	7	8
37	9	10	11	12	13	14	15
38	16	17	18	19	20	21	22
39	23	24	25	26	27	28	29
40	30						

September

2 Monday

Labor Day (US)

3 Tuesday

4 Wednesday

September

5 Thursday

_____
_____
_____
_____
_____
_____
_____
_____
_____
_____
_____
_____
_____
_____
_____
_____
_____
_____
_____
_____
_____
_____
_____
_____
_____

6 Friday

_____
_____
_____
_____
_____
_____
_____
_____
_____
_____
_____
_____
_____
_____
_____
_____
_____
_____
_____
_____
_____
_____

7 Saturday

_____
_____
_____
_____
_____
_____
_____
_____
_____
_____
_____

8 Sunday

_____
_____
_____
_____
_____
_____
_____
_____
_____

Wk	M	T	W	T	F	S	S
35							1
36	2	3	4	5	6	7	8
37	9	10	11	12	13	14	15
38	16	17	18	19	20	21	22
39	23	24	25	26	27	28	29
40	30						

September

9 Monday

10 Tuesday

11 Wednesday

September

12 Thursday

anesh Chaturthi ends

13 Friday

14 Saturday

15 Sunday

Wk	M	T	W	T	F	S	S
35							1
36	2	3	4	5	6	7	8
37	9	10	11	12	13	14	15
38	16	17	18	19	20	21	22
39	23	24	25	26	27	28	29
40	30						

September

16 Monday

17 Tuesday

18 Wednesday

September

19 Thursday

_____
_____
_____
_____
_____
_____
_____
_____
_____
_____
_____
_____
_____
_____
_____
_____
_____
_____
_____
_____
_____
_____
_____
_____
_____
_____

20 Friday

_____
_____
_____
_____
_____
_____
_____
_____
_____
_____
_____
_____
_____
_____
_____
_____
_____
_____
_____
_____
_____
_____
_____

21 Saturday

International Day of Peace (United Nations)

_____
_____
_____
_____
_____
_____
_____

22 Sunday

_____
_____
_____
_____
_____
_____
_____
_____
_____
_____
_____
_____

Wk	M	T	W	T	F	S	S
35							1
36	2	3	4	5	6	7	8
37	9	10	11	12	13	14	15
38	16	17	18	19	20	21	22
39	23	24	25	26	27	28	29
40	30						

September

23 Monday

24 Tuesday

25 Wednesday

September

26 Thursday

27 Friday

28 Saturday

Muharram ends at sunset

29 Sunday

Rosh Hashanah begins at sunset

New Zealand Daylight Saving Time begins

Navratri begins

Wk	M	T	W	T	F	S	S
35							1
36	2	3	4	5	6	7	8
37	9	10	11	12	13	14	15
38	16	17	18	19	20	21	22
39	23	24	25	26	27	28	29
40	30						

WID YE BELIEVE IT?

Horace's Amazing Facts

HORACE
THE BLACK BOX IN AN AEROPLANE IS IN FACT ORANGE.

JOE
"MAYBE IT WIS MADE BY A DUNDEE UNITED SUPPORTER."

HORACE
THERE ARE SOME WASPS THAT MAK HONEY.

BAIRN
"THON'S NOTHIN'! MY MAW MAKS JAM."

HORACE
IF YE CROSS A FEMALE ZEBRA WI' A MALE HORSE, THE OFFSPRING'S CA'ED A HEBRA.

TWIN
"WHIT DAE YE GET IF YE CROSS A TURKEY WI' AN OCTOPUS?"

MAW
"DRUMSTICKS FOR A' THE FAMILY!"

HORACE
THE AVERAGE TEMPERATURE ON NEPTUNE IS -200C.

PAW
"I COULD THOLE THAT – I'VE BEEN ON THE BEACH AT AIBERDEEN IN MY SWIMMING TRUNKS!"

October

The Bairns dress up for Hallowe'en –
They want to go oot guisin'.
But Gran'paw too – whit can this mean?
The answer's quite surprisin'.

30 Monday

1 Tuesday

Rosh Hashanah ends at sunset

2 Wednesday

October

3 Thursday

_____
_____
_____
_____
_____
_____
_____
_____
_____
_____
_____
_____
_____
_____
_____
_____
_____
_____
_____
_____
_____
_____
_____
_____
_____
_____

4 Friday

_____
_____
_____
_____
_____
_____
_____
_____
_____
_____
_____
_____
_____
_____
_____
_____
_____
_____
_____
_____
_____
_____

5 Saturday

_____
_____
_____
_____
_____
_____
_____
_____

6 Sunday

Australian Daylight Saving Time begins

_____
_____
_____
_____
_____
_____
_____
_____

Wk	M	T	W	T	F	S	S
40		1	2	3	4	5	6
41	7	8	9	10	11	12	13
42	14	15	16	17	18	19	20
43	21	22	23	24	25	26	27
44	28	29	30	31			

October

7 Monday

_____

_____

_____

_____

_____

_____

_____

_____

_____

_____

_____

_____

_____

_____

_____

_____

_____

_____

_____

_____

_____

_____

_____

_____

_____

8 Tuesday

Yom Kippur begins at sunset

Navratri ends

_____

_____

_____

_____

_____

_____

_____

_____

_____

_____

_____

_____

_____

_____

_____

_____

_____

_____

_____

_____

_____

_____

_____

9 Wednesday

_____

_____

_____

_____

_____

_____

_____

_____

_____

_____

_____

_____

_____

_____

_____

_____

_____

_____

_____

_____

_____

_____

_____

_____

October

10 Thursday

rld Porridge Day

_____

_____

_____

_____

_____

_____

_____

_____

_____

_____

_____

_____

_____

_____

_____

_____

_____

_____

_____

_____

_____

_____

11 Friday

_____

_____

_____

_____

_____

_____

_____

_____

_____

_____

_____

_____

_____

_____

_____

_____

_____

_____

_____

_____

12 Saturday

_____

_____

_____

_____

_____

_____

_____

_____

13 Sunday

Sukkot begins at sunset

_____

_____

_____

_____

_____

_____

_____

_____

_____

_____

Wk	M	T	W	T	F	S	S
40		1	2	3	4	5	6
41	7	8	9	10	11	12	13
42	14	15	16	17	18	19	20
43	21	22	23	24	25	26	27
44	28	29	30	31			

October

14 Monday

Columbus Day (US)

15 Tuesday

16 Wednesday

October

7 Thursday

18 Friday

19 Saturday

20 Sunday

Sukkot ends at sunset

Wk	M	T	W	T	F	S	S
40		1	2	3	4	5	6
41	7	8	9	10	11	12	13
42	14	15	16	17	18	19	20
43	21	22	23	24	25	26	27
44	28	29	30	31			

October

21 **Monday**

22 **Tuesday**

23 **Wednesday**

October

24 Thursday

25 Friday

26 Saturday

27 Sunday

British Summer Time ends

Diwali begins

Wk	M	T	W	T	F	S	S
40		1	2	3	4	5	6
41	7	8	9	10	11	12	13
42	14	15	16	17	18	19	20
43	21	22	23	24	25	26	27
44	28	29	30	31			

October

28 Monday

29 Tuesday

30 Wednesday

November

Cauld winds and rain can mak ye ill.
It really can be cruel.
One mighty sneeze caused by the chill
Means Grandpaw must eat gruel.

FAITHERS O' INVENTION

THE REFRIGERATION SYSTEM
Was invented by Hamilton man, William Cullen (1710 – 1790) in 1748.

October / November

31 Thursday

allowe'en

wali ends

1 Friday

All Saints' Day

2 Saturday

All Souls' Day

3 Sunday

Daylight Saving Time ends (US, Can)

Wk	M	T	W	T	F	S	S
44					1	2	3
45	4	5	6	7	8	9	10
46	11	12	13	14	15	16	17
47	18	19	20	21	22	23	24
48	25	26	27	28	29	30	

November

4 Monday

5 Tuesday

Guy Fawkes Night (UK)

6 Wednesday

November

7 Thursday

_____
_____
_____
_____
_____
_____
_____
_____
_____
_____
_____
_____
_____
_____
_____
_____
_____
_____
_____
_____
_____
_____
_____
_____
_____
_____
_____

8 Friday

_____
_____
_____
_____
_____
_____
_____
_____
_____
_____
_____
_____
_____
_____
_____
_____
_____
_____
_____
_____
_____
_____
_____
_____
_____

9 Saturday

_____
_____
_____
_____
_____
_____
_____
_____

10 Sunday

Remembrance Sunday

_____
_____
_____
_____
_____
_____
_____
_____
_____
_____

Wk	M	T	W	T	F	S	S
44					1	2	3
45	4	5	6	7	8	9	10
46	11	12	13	14	15	16	17
47	18	19	20	21	22	23	24
48	25	26	27	28	29	30	

November

11 Monday

Remembrance Day

Veterans Day (US)

12 Tuesday

13 Wednesday

Robert Louis Stevenson Day

November

14 Thursday

_____
_____
_____
_____
_____
_____
_____
_____
_____
_____
_____
_____
_____
_____
_____
_____
_____
_____
_____
_____
_____
_____
_____
_____

15 Friday

_____
_____
_____
_____
_____
_____
_____
_____
_____
_____
_____
_____
_____
_____
_____
_____
_____
_____
_____

16 Saturday

_____
_____
_____
_____
_____
_____
_____
_____

17 Sunday

_____
_____
_____
_____
_____
_____
_____
_____
_____

Wk	M	T	W	T	F	S	S
44					1	2	3
45	4	5	6	7	8	9	10
46	11	12	13	14	15	16	17
47	18	19	20	21	22	23	24
48	25	26	27	28	29	30	

November

18 Monday

19 Tuesday

20 Wednesday

November

21 Thursday

_____
_____
_____
_____
_____
_____
_____
_____
_____
_____
_____
_____
_____
_____
_____
_____
_____
_____
_____
_____
_____
_____
_____
_____
_____
_____

22 Friday

_____
_____
_____
_____
_____
_____
_____
_____
_____
_____
_____
_____
_____
_____
_____
_____
_____
_____
_____
_____
_____
_____

23 Saturday

_____
_____
_____
_____
_____
_____
_____

24 Sunday

_____
_____
_____
_____
_____
_____
_____
_____
_____
_____

Wk	M	T	W	T	F	S	S
44					1	2	3
45	4	5	6	7	8	9	10
46	11	12	13	14	15	16	17
47	18	19	20	21	22	23	24
48	25	26	27	28	29	30	

November

25 Monday

26 Tuesday

27 Wednesday

December

The bairns a' love their Christmas toys.
Auld Santa's got it right.
The adults, though, don't share their joys –
It's three o'clock at night!

MAW BROON'S RECIPES

Maw's Fudge

YE'LL NEED:
8" square tin
baking paper
a wee glass o' cauld
water
large non-stick
saucepan

115g unsalted butter
450g soft brown sugar
397g tin o' condensed
milk
1 teaspoon vanilla
extract
150ml milk

WHIT TAE DAE:
1. Grease and line the 8" square tin.
2. In a large, non-stick saucepan, gently heat the butter, sugar, condensed milk, vanilla extract and milk for around 15 minutes. Watch the bairns dinnae pinch any o' the condensed milk.
3. Be careful tae stir occasionally tae stop the mixture sticking tae the foot o' the pan and tae stop it from burning.
4. The mixture is ready when a soft ball is formed when a spoonful is dropped intae a glass o' cauld water.
5. Remove from the heat and beat well wi' a wooden spoon for around 10 minutes or until the mixture has thickened a fair bit.
6. Pour the mixture intae your prepared tin and allow tae cool completely.
7. Remove from tin and cut intae squares.

"Substitute vanilla for any flavour o' yer choice for a wee twist.

Alternatively, add 100g of chocolate chips, chopped nuts or dried fruit - lovely!"

November / December

28 Thursday

...nksgiving Day (US)

29 Friday

30 Saturday

St. Andrew's Day

1 Sunday

Advent Sunday

Wk	M	T	W	T	F	S	S
48							1
49	2	3	4	5	6	7	8
50	9	10	11	12	13	14	15
51	16	17	18	19	20	21	22
52	23	24	25	26	27	28	29
1	30	31					

December

2 Monday

_____
_____
_____
_____
_____
_____
_____
_____
_____
_____
_____
_____
_____
_____
_____
_____
_____
_____
_____
_____
_____
_____
_____
_____
_____

3 Tuesday

_____
_____
_____
_____
_____
_____
_____
_____
_____
_____
_____
_____
_____
_____
_____
_____
_____
_____
_____
_____
_____
_____
_____
_____
_____

4 Wednesday

_____
_____
_____
_____
_____
_____
_____
_____
_____
_____
_____
_____
_____
_____
_____
_____
_____
_____
_____
_____
_____
_____
_____
_____
_____

December

5 Thursday

_____
_____
_____
_____
_____
_____
_____
_____
_____
_____
_____
_____
_____
_____
_____
_____
_____
_____
_____
_____
_____
_____
_____
_____

6 Friday

_____
_____
_____
_____
_____
_____
_____
_____
_____
_____
_____
_____
_____
_____
_____
_____
_____
_____
_____

7 Saturday

_____
_____
_____
_____
_____
_____
_____
_____
_____

8 Sunday

_____
_____
_____
_____
_____
_____
_____
_____
_____
_____

Wk	M	T	W	T	F	S	S
48							1
49	2	3	4	5	6	7	8
50	9	10	11	12	13	14	15
51	16	17	18	19	20	21	22
52	23	24	25	26	27	28	29
1	30	31					

December

9 Monday

10 Tuesday

Human Rights Day

11 Wednesday

December

12 Thursday

_____
_____
_____
_____
_____
_____
_____
_____
_____
_____
_____
_____
_____
_____
_____
_____
_____
_____
_____
_____
_____
_____
_____

13 Friday

_____
_____
_____
_____
_____
_____
_____
_____
_____
_____
_____
_____
_____
_____
_____
_____
_____
_____

14 Saturday

_____
_____
_____
_____
_____
_____
_____
_____
_____
_____

15 Sunday

_____
_____
_____
_____
_____
_____
_____
_____
_____
_____

Wk	M	T	W	T	F	S	S
48							1
49	2	3	4	5	6	7	8
50	9	10	11	12	13	14	15
51	16	17	18	19	20	21	22
52	23	24	25	26	27	28	29
1	30	31					

December

16 Monday

17 Tuesday

18 Wednesday

December

19 Thursday

20 Friday

21 Saturday

22 Sunday

Hanukkah begins at sunset

Winter Solstice

Wk	M	T	W	T	F	S	S
48							1
49	2	3	4	5	6	7	8
50	9	10	11	12	13	14	15
51	16	17	18	19	20	21	22
52	23	24	25	26	27	28	29
1	30	31					

December

23 Monday

24 Tuesday

Christmas Eve

25 Wednesday

Christmas Day, holiday

December

26 Thursday

Boxing Day, holiday

27 Friday

28 Saturday

29 Sunday

Wk	M	T	W	T	F	S	S
48							1
49	2	3	4	5	6	7	8
50	9	10	11	12	13	14	15
51	16	17	18	19	20	21	22
52	23	24	25	26	27	28	29
1	30	31					

December / January

30 Monday

Hanukkah ends at sunset

_____
_____
_____
_____
_____
_____
_____
_____
_____
_____
_____
_____
_____
_____
_____
_____
_____
_____
_____
_____
_____
_____
_____
_____
_____
_____
_____
_____
_____

31 Tuesday

Hogmanay (New Year's Eve)

_____
_____
_____
_____
_____
_____
_____
_____
_____
_____
_____
_____
_____
_____
_____
_____
_____
_____
_____
_____
_____
_____
_____
_____
_____
_____
_____
_____
_____

1 Wednesday

New Year's Day, holiday

_____
_____
_____
_____
_____
_____
_____
_____
_____
_____
_____
_____
_____
_____
_____
_____
_____
_____
_____
_____
_____
_____
_____
_____
_____
_____
_____
_____
_____

Merry Christmas and Happy New Year from The Broons!

Notes

Notes

....
....
....
....
....
....
....
....
....
....
....
....
....
....
....
....
....
....
....
....

Notes

....

....

....

....

....

....

....

....

....

....

....

....

....

....

Notes

....
....
....
....
....
....
....
....
....
....
....
....
....
....

First published 2018
by Black & White Publishing Ltd
Nautical House, 104 Commercial Street, Edinburgh, EH6 6NF
ISBN: 978 1 910230 55 8

www.thebroons.com

A CIP catalogue record for this book is available from the British Library.

Typeset by Creative Link, Haddington
Printed and bound by Opolgraf, Poland